Powerful Words To U

Re- Educating God's

Written By:

Isaiah Donaldson

Jr

Use blank sheets to take notes on scriptures:

Introduction

You have the power to be whoever you want to be. No one can tell you that you can't be. Won't be. Or shouldn't be. If you want it, you can have it.

If you say it, then it shall be heard. If you believe it, you can accomplish it. You have the power that is within all.The energy that was all is all, and will forever be all. Don't forget because of the doubters. Don't forget because of the non accomplishers. Remember what the word says.

Jeremiah chapter 29, verse 11-14.

-Don't forget. I know the plans that I have for you, said the Lord, your God plans for welfare and

not for evil. To give you a good future and hope. You will call for me and pray to me and trust me I will hear you. When you search for me with all of your heart, you will find me. You will find me, said the Lord and I will surely restore your fortune.-

Don't you ever feel as if he doesn't hear you. Remember his strength and let him fight your battle. Your neighbors will talk. Your friends will laugh behind your back. Your ex will hate. That's normal.

When people know that you can be better, but don't want you to. They will say whatever they want to take you off of your game. Don't let them win. God knows your potential, and so do you.

Trust him and watch what he does. Believe in yourself and watch how he will reveal your powers right in front of you. Did you know that your powers come from within? Smile and stop acting like you want to be sad.

Smile and stop acting like you want to be mad. If you want to be happy, then be happy! It's simple. You can do whatever you want to do. What is stopping you from being happy? What is stopping you from having fun? What is stopping you from feeling loved?

It's not him! It's not her! If you are unhappy, it is you that's frowning. Stop it! Snap out of it. You're walking around here pretending as if you aren't special. It's you that forgot to be happy because of what someone else said to you.

It is you that is forgetting how much God loves you. You better get it together! Don't you ever forget what the word says.

Hebrews chapter 13, verse 8-9

-You do know that Jesus Christ is the same yesterday and today and forever. Don't be turned away by diverse and strange teachings. It is good for

the heart to be strengthened by grace, not by foods which have not benefited those devoted to them.-

Hebrews chapter 3, verse 5-7

-I will never leave you or forsake you. So you can say confidently. The Lord is my helper. I will not fear. What can man do to me? Remember the leaders. They spoke the word of God. Pay attention and consider their outcome of the way of life and imitate their faith.-

<u>Chapter 1</u>

OVERCOMING DEPRESSION:
GOD'S GOT YOUR BACK

Today is not tomorrow. Today is not yesterday. Why did you wake up and frown? You just opened your eyes. Why didn't you say thank God for waking me up? Thank you God, for giving me another day to live my beautiful life.

Aren't you happy to see another day? I know you've had problems in the past, but you have to move on. What happened yesterday can't be changed. What happened last year can't be edited.

You have to know in your heart, in your mind, and in your spirit that you can and will have a better day. Do you believe in yourself? Do you know how awesome you are? Don't you know how great you are?

Better yet, don't you know how great the creator is? Matter of fact, let's just sit here and talk. Do you believe in God? Be honest. In your mind. I won't judge you. I can't and I won't. Be real with yourself. Do you really believe in God?

What is God to you? Before you keep going throughout your day with that mindset that you have. I want you to be honest with yourself. Is there a God? Did God create the world? Or did The Big Bang Theory happen?

I'm not telling you what to believe, but what I will tell you is what I believe. I believe that you're a great person and you can do better than you did in the past. I know you can. Stop frowning because of what happened before.

Today is a new day. You should be happy. That you were given another day to be better. Don't be ashamed of your past. Use it as a learning experience, not a failure. You didn't fail, you experienced.

You didn't fail. You went through something. You didn't lose. You learned. You have to believe in yourself. You have to believe in better. You have to learn from your mistakes so that you don't make them again.

Stop feeling bad for the past. You're just you. You're not God. Only God is perfect. You were created to live, learn, decide, attempt, succeed, prosper, desire, want, need, love, and more.

That comes with the territory. The land is not yours. The land is his and he will test you. Don't fail the test. Don't think more than you should. Don't doubt yourself.

Don't underestimate the power of God. You have to know that things will get better. Life isn't that easy to just feel as if you will always win. It's so hard sometimes.

You won't just get everything done on your own. That doesn't mean hold on to those bitter feelings of the past. If you get stressed out about something, pray and know that God will hear you.

Believe that he will help you. Then move on. Why give your belief to God, but don't trust him to help you? That doesn't make sense. If you had a bad day. If you went through something bad. If you went through the struggle. Pray about it and know that the one you believe in has your back.

You better know that God heard you last night. You better know that God will be there for you. You better not doubt the God that you chose to believe in! You chose to believe in God, didn't you?

Well, you better remember how powerful God is. Don't say you believe, but act like you don't. If you believe in God, then you know God has your back.

1 Peter chapter 5, verse 5-10.

-You do know that God opposes the ones who are proud, but gives grace to the humble. Humble yourself under the mighty hand of God, so that at the proper time He may exalt you. Putting all of your anxieties on him because he truly cares about you. Be sober in your mind. Pay attention. The devil wanders around just looking for someone to attack. Resist him. Stay prayed up and faithful, knowing that the same kind of sufferings are being experienced by people all over the world, not just you. You better know that after you suffer a little bit, God, who has given you eternal glory in Jesus Christ, will hear you accept you, love you, strengthen you, and establish you.-

AMEN!

Chapter 2

Monday

My neighbor loves me more than my own brothers. Is that OK? To be honest, sometimes I feel like the strangers in the community like me more than the people in my family.

I used to feel so alone, angry, sad, and depressed. All of the brain shaking, unpeaceful emotions that there are. I would try to talk to them about my goals and they would downplay my ideas instantly. I'm talking so fast.

I remember I told my mother about my plan to start a group home, it's a non profitable organization. That would involve me sheltering a bunch of elderly people in need. Some of them may have had mental health issues and the others medical issues.

I've always had a business mind and that one was a double plus for me. I would have been getting paid to help the elderly. I love helping people and I like to earn money, so to be able to do both at the same time was exciting.

When I came and told her, she immediately told me that she didn't like my business plan and she advised me to just get a regular low paying job. I remember hearing her say, why don't you just get a regular job and work your way up like I did? I was disgusted by her answer because to me, I know that she didn't even like her struggle that she has just now overcome.

I didn't like her situation. Just because she is comfortable now doesn't mean I want it to be like her. I want more for myself. I want to be better. There is nothing wrong with wanting to do better.

Most of the people that I know, befriended, spoke to, or went to school with have that same problem. No one wants the next person to end up better than them. It seems like once you show someone that you have the potential to do better, they turn their backs on you.

Why are people so envious of each other? Why don't they just have a genuine acceptance for someone else's passion? Why don't they just embrace each other's dreams? Why don't they just support each other?

It's very childish, but very common. We all need someone in our corner. Do you have the love and support that you truly desire in life? Do you have the good feedback that you desire when you express your plans to others? Do they tell you congratulations when you accomplish something, or do they look at you with jealousy in their eyes?

If they don't, it's because they are jealous. They are humans trying to live their life the same way you are trying to live yours. It is natural for a human to think like a human. Don't let it bother you, just continue to shine, Queen. Continue to push yourself king.

Trust me, you can do it. I believe in you. Don't you? I'm on your side because I know better. You can be what you want because God has your back. He is on your side. I'm on your side. Jesus Christ is on your side.

Don't worry about what someone else's struggle brought them. Your struggle will bring your victory. Your victory will happen if you believe. You have to stop putting so many thoughts into what a man or woman speaks with their negative tongue and more into the positive words of God.

God is all you need. He will allow you to prosper based upon his loyalty alone. God is so loyal that no person can be there for you more than him. He will always have your back.

Don't wander to a man for answers. Don't pour out your heart to a woman for support. Go to God. God loves you. God will honor your relationship more than any male or female ever can.

If you tell a person that you are wiser than them they will get offended. If you express that your goal is to have a bigger house than your friend, they will get jealous. If you tell people about your goals, they will make them sound so unaccomplished just to discourage you from achieving them.

People are so petty, but not God. God will hear your goals and help you achieve them. God will hear your wants and give them to you. God will see your struggle and bless you for not giving up on him. Just him! He is the one to go to. Listen to this.

Psalms Chapter 118, verse 6-13.

-God is on your side. You better not be scared. What can a man do to you? He is on your side as your helper, so look for a victory when it comes to those who hate you. It's better to take refuge in the Lord than to trust a man. It's better to take refuge in the Lord than to trust a woman. People will surround you. In the Lord's name, cut them off. They will surround you like bees. They will go out like a fire blown with horns. Cut them off in the name of the Lord. You will be pushed hard so that you can fall, but God will help you.-

Do you understand your gift? Do you understand your talent? Do you understand your purpose? Trust me, you have one. You're not just a bum. You're not just an addict. You're not just a person that works and dies.

You are more than what you know. That's exactly why they don't like you. They see your potential. They know you will be greater than you are now. Just think about it. If you put your mind to it then you can do it.

Do you think God made it possible for you to have life for no reason. You better smile and figure out your reason. Don't waste the great life that God gave you because you listened to the devil tell you otherwise.

That person that told you that you can't do it is filled with hatred. That woman that told you that it won't work, is filled with jealousy. They can see your greatness. Why can't you?

God gave you that great spirit. You better appreciate it. Don't you see that they are just waiting for you to mess up so that they can laugh at your downfall? Don't let them tell you that you can't do it.

God said you can. You need to tell the truth. Not just your truth. Our truth that God made true. Repeat this scripture twice now.

Psalms, chapter 119, verse 1-8.

Blessed are the ones whose ways are blameless, who walk in the law of God. Are the ones who keep his testimonies. Who seek him with their entire heart. Who also does no wrong.   Just walk in his ways. "You have commanded your laws to be followed. Oh, let my ways be steadfast and keep your statues. I will not be put to shame. I am paying attention to all of your commandments. I will praise you forever with a genuine heart when I learn your righteous rules. I will keep your statues.   Please do not leave me or forsaken me."

AMEN!

Chapter 3

Tuesday

LOL! Yesterday I was talking to my friend about their relationship and they were telling me how awful things were going. She told me that they argued about nothing major at first.

It all started over a simple conversation about which celebrity had more money. Now of course, when she told me, it was so petty that I shook my head so many times.

I listened to her for 10 minutes explain how it went from which celebrity made more money, to where they were from, to why they were so rich, to which one of them was broke.

I was shocked, but I kept listening, she told me that, he said. "Now I see why you're broke, because of the way you think." Then they argued about how he was better than her baby father and why her husband left her.

Then after a while I cut her off and said. "So you guys started the conversation about people that neither one of you knew, then began arguing. then you went on to picking at each other?" She said, "yes because he is so stupid."

Then I cut her off again and asked her, "Well, what did you say about him?" Then she said to be honest. "I told him that he should be happy that his mother has helped him his whole life because ain't no other woman going to accept him."

He is an egoistic, selfish man, she said. Then I laughed and gave her a hug. "First off, calm down. You get too excited about the littlest things." I went through the back and forth with my ex too. It happens.

It's normal, but disagreements and petty disputes should always have a limit, I told her.

My baby mother never understood that. She would always turn a petty argument into something big. She is a toxic person. Every person is not fit to be that close to you. You can't allow everyone to be so close to you that they know all of the personal things about you that they can use to control your emotions.

She began to cry. Then she looked up at me and said. "I miss my ex-husband. Men that I date are nothing like him." I didn't say or think anything. I just hugged her again and held her tight until she stopped crying.

When she left I called my wife and said baby, "I love you so much. Thank you for being more than just my girlfriend. You are like my best friend, my daughter and my sister wrapped in one form."

Only God can be responsible for bringing such a woman into my life. I blew her a kiss and then hung up the phone. I walked over to the couch and sat down. I remember the verbal abuse that I went through in my previous relationships.

We always bumped heads because in all honesty, we weren't meant for each other. We weren't meant to grow forever. Not every relationship is meant to be forever.

Most relationships are just opportunities to gain some type of learning experience. There are so many beautiful women in the world that go through relationship after relationship and still have not learned the problem yet.

It blows my mind, but I understand. Beautiful women, stop underestimating your power. A lot of women accept bad, unhealthy relationships. Why? Because they overlook the lesson that God has placed in front of them to learn.

A boyfriend is just that. A boy-friend. He is not the one that you give your all to. He is not the one you give your heart to. He is just a boy-friend. Stop depending on friends. They will always let you down. They weren't placed in your life to be depended on.

They were placed in your life by God to help you get to the next step in your life. That's it. Your children are the future. Give them your attention. Your goals are your future. Your success is your future.

Stop putting friends above your children. Stop putting friends above your success. Stop putting friends above the purpose that God gave you. In order to get to where you need to go.

You have to take the proper steps. Stop moving backwards. Love yourself. Learn from your mistakes. Every experience in life is to make you a better, stronger you. God wants you to be the best you that you can be.

Before you can be the best you, you have to be and acknowledge the worse you. You can't just be perfect. You can't just be great. You have to learn how to be great.

You have to learn how to be strong. You have to learn how to be better. Take your time and understand what role you played in that unhealthy <u>friendship</u>.

Trust me, you will understand how to be better., if you reflect on your actions and learn from them. Change your bad habits and you will create good ones. Change your bad ways and you will create good ones.

There is nothing wrong with you. You are awesome. You are better than what your ex-boy-friend knew. You are of the people. The people who are God's chosen. Royalty is in your bloodline.

Before a little girl can be a grown woman. She has to grow. It takes time to be great. It takes time to be at your best. God has chosen you to be a queen, but first you have to learn how to be a Princess.

A princess is not born a queen. She is born to be one. She is taught and trained and prepared. The same comes with being a wife. You have to learn what a wife is. How a wife responds. How a wife talks.

It's not easy, but it's not hard. You have to pay attention and learn. The way you treat a boy-friend that will come and go as he chooses, is not the same way you treat a husband who is intended to stay forever.

Always remember, a boy-friend is designed to be temporary. That's why you use him to learn from. Use him to get to the next step. The next level. The next level is supposed to be better.

Stop letting yourself feel bad because the boy-friend is not perfect. He will never be perfect. He will never be great. He is not supposed to be. Look at what God will give you. Look at what God can give you.

Why are you upset over a jealous man? Why are you depressed about an abusive boy-friend? Why are you feeling down? Because of what a temporary boy-friend said to you? Wasn't he designed to be temporary?

Let him go in peace and reflect on what was unpeaceful. Let him walk away so that you can learn how to be better for who is better. Trust me. You don't want to waste years being sad and miss out on being happy because you weren't focused.

Because you weren't ready. Get ready. Be ready. Your husband is waiting.

Isaiah chapter 54, verse 4-8.

- Have No Fear. You will not be ashamed. Be not confused or you will not be disgraced, for you will forget the shame of your children and the experience of a widow you will not remember. Your creator is your husband. The Lord of Host is his name, and the Holy One of Israel is your Redeemer. He is God of the whole entire earth. The Lord has called you like a bride, deserted and grieved in spirit. Like the wife of children when it's cast off says you're God. For a second I left you, but with sincere compassion I will be back for you and gather you. I left you and hid my face out of anger, but with everlasting love I will have compassion on you, says the Lord your God.-

Get used to claiming God as your husband and trust me, you will learn how to be the best you. Stop focusing on a temporary boy-friend and focus on the bigger picture. Your permanent husband is waiting for you.

Chapter 4

Wednesday

These are the words of a great preacher.He is the son of David, King of Jerusalem.

Ecclesiastes Chapter 2, verse 15-18.

- I thought to myself and said in my heart with great emotion. What will happen to the fool, will also happen to me. I've been so wise and prideful, but why? This is so bad. For the fool is the same as the wise. There is no length to the remembrance, because when it is all over, all will be forgotten. Both the wise and the fool will one day die. I started to hate my life because what I have done on earth was grievous to me. For all is still bad and a striving after the fleshly

things. So I hated what I have earned from work when I realized that I could not take it with me and would have to leave it to another man.-

Some people are rich. Some people are poor. What is gained in life will be lost in death. Remember to be happy and appreciate what you have. You can have everything and not be happy inside. You can have everything and take life for granted. I suggest that you love your life more.

God is a jealous God, but he is a giving God. He will give you everything that your heart desires because he loves you. Please remember him and be humble. Some people get their blessings in life and forget that they are blessings.

Don't point at someone else and think wrongly of him because you have more. Don't laugh at her because she has less than you. Help your neighbor. Help the stranger. Take a liking to the person that is doing good.

The responsibility of a successful person is to give back to God's children. That is your responsibility. Bless the rest so that God will continue to bless you. We have to support each other.

Support that young boy who is selling water on the side of the road because he is willing to work for his food, not laugh at him because he doesn't have the best job in the world. Remember, he could be robbing you instead of asking you to support his wants.

Don't get prideful and forget that God has blessed you with the things that you have. Don't get too happy and think that you did things on your own.

Give God his thanks, because it was him that made it possible for you to have it in the first place. We will all die one day. Stop being selfish and thinking highly of yourself because the truth is.The millionaire can't take $10 million to heaven with him.

It will stay in his bank account for his children to spend. It will stay in that safe that he left it in until someone finds it. The millionaire.The thousandaire.

The hundredaire will still be who they are until they die, but God has the power to take it when he is ready.

Be humble people and love your successful responsibility as well as he who made it possible.

The words of a great preacher.The son of David, king of Jerusalem.

Ecclesiastes chapter 2 verse 24-26

- Out of all the good, there is nothing greater for a person than to eat and drink and be happy for what they have earned. I remembered. That it comes from God. Who can eat and who can enjoy is God's decision. Those who pleases Him. God has given great wisdom, joy, and knowledge, but those who sin. He has given the business of collecting all only to give to the one that pleases God. This is also bad and striving after the wind.-

What time is it? Is it your time to learn or is it your time to teach? Is it your time to enjoy or is it your time to earn? Stop being impatient because you don't have it right now. Stop being angry because what you want didn't happen when you wanted it to. Stop fussing because it hasn't come fast enough.

If you understand how time works, you will understand that patience comes with success. You will be successful. Just keep going. You will get that new car. Just keep working. You will get that house. Just keep trying.

Trust me, you will have that successful business. Just keep learning and taking the steps that you need to. You can be whatever you want in time. Nothing happens without the proper time and conditions for it to be able to happen.

What time is it? Time to grind or time to shine? What day is it? Is it a work day or is it the day to rest? Stop being so impatient. You got this. Don't you believe it? Don't you want it? Do you deserve it?

If you do want God to give it to you. Stop complaining about what hasn't happened yet. Be patient and remember that God loves you and is watching you.

Don't ask him for something and be upset that he didn't give it to you that second. He had so many others to please. He had so many others to bless. Wait your turn.

The words of a great preacher.The son of David, king of Jerusalem.

Ecclesiastes chapter 3 verse 1-13

- There is a reason for everything and a time for everything on earth. There is a time to be born and there is a time to die. There is a time to kill and there is a time to heal. There is a time to be sad and a time

to be happy. There is a time to embrace and a time to refrain from embracing at all. There is a time to gain and there is a time to lose. There is a time to be quiet and there is a time to speak. There is a time to love and there is a time to hate. What does the worker truly gain? I have noticed the business that God has given to the children is to be busy. He has created everything nice and beautiful in time. He has also put eternity into Man's heart. But he cannot find out what God has done from the beginning to the end. I know now that there is nothing better for anyone to do but to be happy and to continue to do good as long as they live. They should just eat and drink and take pleasure in what they have earned. This is the gift that God gives to man.-

Chapter 5

Thursday

Words from the first letter of Paul to the Corinthians.

1 Corinthians chapter 3, verse 8-11.

- The person that plants in the field and the one that waters the plants are the same and they both will be paid for their work, for they are God's workers. You are God's field and God's building. Like a skilled master builder, one has laid a foundation and someone else will build upon it. Each person has to do their part and take care of how it is built, but no one can lay a foundation other than the one that is laid, which is Jesus Christ.-

Corinthians chapter 3, verse 16-21.

- Don't you know the truth? That you are God's temple and that God's spirit dwells in you. If someone destroys God's temple, God will destroy him. For God's temple is holy, and believe me, you are God's temple. Do not anyone deceive himself. If anyone around you thinks that he is wise, he will become a fool so that he can become wise because the wisdom of the earth is foolish to God, and he catches the wise in their craftiness. Remember, the Lord knows the thoughts of the wise, so be sure not to boast. For all things are yours through Christ.-

Today is the day that you should look around at what you have. You have worked so hard to be able to say you have earned. Are you happy now? Are you proud of yourself?

Well, you should be. Everything that you have, you have. Therefore value what you have done. Value your work. No matter what you've earned, remember that you worked for it. Get it together and be proud of yourself. Don't frown or say this is not enough.

Don't say I don't have what I want. You have what you worked for! If it's something more that you want, simply work more. Don't complain if you have enough.

Don't boast or brag to bring down another that has less. Accept your earnings with a smile and appreciation. You have earned the right to say. "I'm happy that I have, but you don't have the right to say. I have more than you. Don't do this to your friends. Don't do this to your family. Don't do this to your enemy.

Just appreciate your position because not only did you work for it, but it was also given to you. God has given you the opportunity to say I worked and I earned. I worked and I have. I worked and I bought.

These statements are the blessings of your work and your struggle. Remember that God can take it away! Live and be happy that you can live. Enjoy your nice things because you will only have them for a short while anyway.

Life is before death but death is still guaranteed. Don't you dare make someone else feel ashamed because they don't have as much as you. Their hearts may be pure.

Don't cancel your next blessing because you bragged and made someone else sad about your previous blessing. That's not fair. Everyone will earn what they have worked for and God is the payer. God is The Giver. God is the blesser.

Appreciate him and you will keep what he has given you. Remember, he is the one that allowed you to have it in the first place.

Respect yourself and don't disrespect the next because we are all God's children and he is paying according to what is worked for and not based upon who is loved more.

__Proverbs chapter 16 verse 1-9__

- The plans and goals that come from the heart are loved by man, but the answer of the tongue and the true word is from the Lord. The ways are pure in the eyes of the man, but the Lord will judge the Spirit. Have faith and commit your work to the Lord, and your goals will come true, for He will establish them. Everything that the Lord has made has its reasons. Even the wicked are for the day of trouble. Everyone that is ignorant and boasts too much in their heart is an abomination to the Lord. Understand he will be punished. By showing love and faith makes up for sin, and by fearing the Lord, you escape the force of evil. When you please the Lord, you will make even your enemies be peaceful with you. Just a little righteousness is holy and better than to be wealthy and dishonest. The feelings, thoughts, emotion and desires of a man's heart plans his way, but the Lord makes his plans accomplishable.-

Give God your heart and all of your business plans, vacation plans, life plans, whatever you want will come true because he loves you and he will bless you with everything that you want and need.

AMEN

<u>Chapter 6</u>

Friday

The words of Paul, the servant of God and also an apostle of Jesus Christ.

Titus chapter 2 verse 2-8

- Men of a certain age are to be strong minded, have dignity, self-control, have a lot of faith and to be filled with love. Women of a certain age should be the same and mature, not as slaves to alcohol or wine. They are to teach good teachings. Train the younger women to love their husbands and children. Have self-control, be pure and honest, working at home, kind and be submissive to their own husbands. That the word of God may not be disobeyed inspiring the younger men to have self-control. You need to be as you should in all respects to be a role model of good works. Show dignity and integrity in your teachings.

Speak right and that which can't be condemned. So that no one, especially an enemy, can have anything evil to say about you.-

Titus chapter 1 v7-8

- Don't be arrogant or quick tempered or an alcoholic or violent or greedy to gain anything. Instead show great hospitality, a lover of good, self controlled, upright, holy and have discipline.-

If no one has told you today, let me let you know something. You are a great person. Sometimes we get caught up in the motions of our day and forget to say the little things. We forget to do the little things, but to be honest with you, sometimes it's the little things that count.

You are wonderful and you need to hear it. You've come a long way. Trust me, it's not easy to be where you are right now. The past issues of yours are still someone else's present issues. The prior addictions of yours, are the death of some.

Not everybody is blessed enough to say. " I am done with the drugs, or I am done with the alcohol, or I am done with cheating, or I am done with clubbing, or I am done with the streets, or I am done with the gangs, or I am done with breaking the law, or I am done trying to please people, or I am done following others, or I am done being unhappy."

You are blessed just because you are done being what you were. Move on with your life. You can do it. You have done it. You are awesome. I hope you are proud of yourself, because you should be.

Your life is like a book. It started off good, then had a drastic turn and the flip of a few pages. It wasn't easy to read. No one saw it coming. You didn't know where it was going, but boom. The twist came and it took a while before it got better.

The good thing is. It got better. I knew it wasn't fun, but you had to gain the experience you have today in order to be the great person you are today. No wonder you are who you are.

Look at what you've overcome. God is so proud of you for being obedient. God is so proud of you for being mindful of your mistakes and finally learning from them. You didn't know that you could do it, but trust me, God knew it.

He had your back this whole time. He knew what would make you, and he knew what would break you. He knew that you would get it together. He tested you over and over again. He watched you fail. He listened to you cry. He listened to you complain.

Just to keep testing you. He put you to the test so that you could fail and learn how not to fail. It's not a game. It's not a fair battle unless you have the proper weapons to defend yourself. We aren't born the best that we can be.

We have to learn to be the best that we can be. You have done all of the losing. All of the complaining. All of the fighting just to look up at the sky and scream to God. "I didn't give up on myself. I didn't give up on you, God. I learned what you wanted me to and I will help the next person overcome."

Do your part in the healing process. We are all broken men and women. We all need fixing. God knows how to fix us, and he knows how to break us. Didn't he fix you? Didn't he fix me?

OK, then God can fix all. I'm here to tell you that he fixed me. God has healed me with his power. With his mercy. With his grace. With his love. I didn't know that I would be here today.

I was drunk for half of my life. Every single day I got drunk. I blacked out. I got arrested. I even woke up in the hospital twice and didn't remember how I got there. It was horrible. I made so many mistakes in life and no one had my back.

I felt alone. No one believed that I could do it. Everyone turned away from me. No one helped me. I turned my life around because I had no other choice.

God called me to be one of his helpers. One of his workers. I work for God now and he has paid me with a better life. I've been sober from alcohol for five years now. I use my experience in alcohol abuse and change lives.

My wife had a really bad alcohol problem when I met her and I used a similar medicine to cure her as little as one month from the day I met her. This isn't a game. This isn't a fair battle unless you have the proper tools to defend yourself, and I have them now.

The devil won't get me. I have taught so many people how to win the battle. This is the responsibility of a changed man. Now it is your responsibility. Give someone the proper weapons to win the battle.

Don't you dare hold on to them. You have been blessed. Now you better help God's people receive their blessing. It's your job as a skilled learner. You have learned from your life.

Now you can teach that beautiful child how to live better. Now you can teach that man how to live better. Now you can teach that young woman how to behave better. God has called upon you to learn the lessons of life in order for you to teach the lessons of life.

You are special because God didn't give up on you and you didn't give up on God? Show some hospitality. Show some love. Show yourself control. Let others see how much discipline you have. You are a walking legend.

You have overcome so much and now God wants to use you as a real life role model. Show the youth what dedication looks like. Show the youth what it looks like to achieve goals in the midst of adversity.

Show the world what God's child looks like. You are wonderful and the world needs to know why. That child needs to know why. That teenager needs to know how. How did God change your life?

How did God help you? How did you overcome it? How did you get to the point of healing? Do you have regrets? What are the steps of fixing your life?

These are the questions that need to be answered, but only by someone that has the answers.

God gave you the answers so that when it's time to help the next, you can. You'll be able to answer these questions truthfully. No one needs a made-up answer. No one needs a fake response, they need the truth.

Only people who have the answers can give the answers. That's why it's important for you to help God's children, because he gave you the answers. Now continue to grow and learn because you have been blessed by God.

You have the answer to the questions because of what you went through. God put you through the test. God put you in the crossfire to make you stronger, not to punish you. All experiences are not punishments.

Learn what you have to so that you can pass the test. You can proudly say that you failed because you can proudly say that you learned how not to fail. It takes time to be great.

It takes time to be better. How long did it take you? How many times did you fail? How many times did you cry? These are the questions that will make it easier for someone else to believe you.

Spread your word with people and God will vouch for you. He is your God and he is watching what you do with your gift. He is watching to see how much you appreciate his blessings. Do not fail the next test. Help yourself. Help the youth. Help the next life just as God helps yours.

The words of Paul, the servant of God and also an apostle of Jesus Christ.

Titus chapter 2 verse 11-15

- Did you see that God's grace is among us? Bring salvation to all the people. He is training us to go away and to not accept ungodliness and earthly passions and to have self-control, live in a straight path and to live in a righteous way. Waiting for hope

and to be blessed by God. He has given himself to redeem us from corruption and the ways of the wicked, and to make us pure, so that we can be of his prized possession and do good deeds. Live righteous and declare this. Exhort and rebuke authority. Do not let anyone disregard who you are.-

Chapter 7

Saturday

Corinthians chapter 10, verse 1-13.

- Be aware, brothers, our fathers were all on earth. They were all baptized to be priests. They all ate the same exact spiritual food. They all drank the same spiritual drink. From Jesus Christ. God wasn't pleased with most of them. Do not desire evil as they did because they were your examples. Don't become idolaters like some of them. Do not indulge in homosexuality as some of them did. Remember, 23,000 of them died in one day. Do not test Christ, because they did and were destroyed. Do not grumble, because they did and were destroyed by the Destroyer. They were the examples and it is written to be read as our instructions. So pay attention and do the right thing unless you want to be punished. Do not become weak to temptation. God is faithful and won't let you be tempted more than you can handle, but the temptation that does tempt you he will provide you with an escape.-

Life is filled with obstacles. Twist and turns, that should be expected. Not all things happen at the right time, but in time of temptation. At a time of adversity. At a time of confusion. At a time of chaos.

Remember what was set out for you? Remember the outcome for those who set down the examples. Pay attention to life. There is a repeated cycle. Life will continue. Life will never bring anything new to life without bringing something old to death.

Pay attention to what was done by the ones before you. Be sure to have role models. Don't worship them, just pay attention to them. Your role model doesn't have to be a rapper. It doesn't have to be a famous actor.

It doesn't have to be your parent. It can be the bus driver that sets a good example for the youth. It can be the older woman down the street that always says nice things to you when you walk past her or the prophets in the Bible.

Pay attention to what is done right and do not mimic what was done wrong, because you know that. It was wrong. When things come into play in life, you will be held responsible for how you handled yourself.

God wants you to be mature. God wants you to be loving. God wants you to be caring. Live your life knowing that God is watching your every move.

If you knew that your mother was standing behind you at every second of the day, would you do wrong right in front of her? Do you think a kid would steal from the store right in front of the police? Do you think a man would smoke weed in front of his probation officer?

Do you think that a criminal would commit a crime right in front of the judge? I don't think so. We as God's people. We, as God's children, should have the same respect for God every second of the day, because he is truly watching us every second.

He is truly staring right at us before, during and after we are tempted to do the wrong thing. How do you think he feels watching us procrastinate when temptation comes for us, only to still make the wrong decision?

The one thing about it is. We know when we are being tempted. We know when we are about to do something wrong. We think about our decision before we make it and then we still fall victim.

This is a sign of weakness. This is wrong and we need to do better. Nothing else should be done except for the right thing. Stop making the wrong decision on purpose. Stop falling for temptation when you know deep down that it is temptation.

This is wrong. You are too good for that. God is too great to look at his children and to watch them do wrong. He doesn't like it, and neither should we.

No, you shouldn't be judged by others, but you should be corrected. Try your best to be like you should and not like you were. Before you knew right, you knew wrong. Before you knew better, you knew worse.

Now that you know better you should think better. You should do better. Don't continue to be fooled. What is the difference between the fooled and the fooled that is fooled knowingly? Cut it out and be the awesome you. All the time because God is always watching you.

Do good and make the right decision all the time because you are expected to and have been commanded to. You have been taught to. What is written is your example?

What is written is your instruction. Use it. Read it. Do as you should because it was placed in writing and put right in front of you. The world is the world. The profits are the messengers. God is the book, and you are the writer. Open your eyes and read the message. Remember the ways of the ones before you as an example. Use the example as your personal instruction pamphlet.

Do better because you know better. Do not be easily tempted by the evil that roams the world. Do not lose because you chose to give into temptation. Do not let the devil win. God is watching you all the time. Do not let God witness you cheat on your husband. Do not let God watch you cheat on your wife.

Do not let God watch you neglect your children. Do not let God watch you abuse your children. Do not let God watch you abuse alcohol. Do not let God watch you abuse drugs. Do not let God watch you fall victim to the devil's temptation.

Luke Chapter 4 verse 1-13

- Jesus is holy in spirit. He walked from the Jordan and was walked by the Spirit into the wilderness. He was tempted by the devil for 40 days and he didn't eat the entire time. He was hungry. The devil told Jesus make this stone turn into bread if you are the Son of God. It has been written, no man should live by bread alone, but by the word of God,

Jesus said. Then the devil being filled with evil took Jesus and showed him the kingdoms of the world fast. He said I will give you all this authority and their glory. It is mine. I can give it to whoever I want to. If you worship me, it will be yours. Then Jesus said get back Satan. It has been written, You shall worship the Lord your God, and you shall only serve him. Then the devil took Jesus to Jerusalem and put him on the top of the temple and said. If you are really the Son of God, jump down. It was written that he will send his angels down to help you. They will lift you up unless you hit your foot against a stone then, Jesus said. You shall not put the Lord your God to test. Then the devil stopped tempting Jesus, and he left until he felt like it was a better time to tempt him.-

I am here to tell you. Brother and sister. Do not fall for the temptation of the devil. Let what was written be the example for you. What was written, be your instructions to rise over the devil's petty temptation. God is watching you.!

AMEN

Chapter 8

Sunday

1st Samuel verse 7

- The Lord is your God, said to Samuel. Do not look at the appearance of someone. You men and women look at people and see them based upon how they look, but the Lord looks at the person and sees what's in their heart.-

Good morning. Good afternoon. Goodnight. Every day should be good. Why wasn't it a good morning? You are alive today. You are not stuck in your sleep forever. You are alive and well. So good morning. Why isn't it a good afternoon? You are still breathing the breath of life.

You were able to smile. You are able to make your reality whatever you want it to be. So good afternoon. Why isn't it a good night?

You are still alive. You do have the chance to pray and ask for forgiveness. You can still talk to God and ask him to make tomorrow better. So goodnight. Stop looking for the bad to say about things and start looking for the good to say.

Life is whatever you make it. Looks can be deceiving. Stop looking at your day and only acknowledging the bad that has happened. Doesn't bad happen to everyone? You also have another side to think about.

There was something good that happened that you are not acknowledging. You are OK unless you tell yourself that you are not. What you see can sometimes deceive you to make you think what you want.

What you think can sometimes deceive you and make you feel a certain type of way. What you have to do is remember everything is not always the way you make it seem. Everything that you see is not always the way you perceive it in your brain.

When some people see me, they see a black gangster with tattoos. When others see me, they see a survivor. When others see me, they see a great father. When others see me, they see a successful man, but how many of them can see my pain?

How many of them can see my struggle? How many of them can see my accomplishments? How many of them can see my dedication? How many of them can see my future?

How many of them can see my heart? I am more than what they see, but yet they use my clothes, my shoes, my appearance as a way to judge me. They use my outer shell to determine who I am. Does it bother me? No, because I know what is in my mind.

I know what's in my heart, and so does God. I put on these clothes to feel comfortable. I put on these shoes to walk. My swag doesn't make me who I am. My mind, heart and spirit is what matters. Their thoughts, their jokes, their suggestions, their opinions don't bother me because they don't matter.

We people have to stop being so naive. Don't look at the wrong things. A person should be judged because of who he is and not what he wears. You are beautiful because of who you are, not because of how much makeup you have on.

You are beautiful because of the way you carry yourself and not because of your designer clothes. I love my wife because of her personality, not because of her skin color. She is a beautiful woman on the inside. She is caring, she is polite.

She is honest. She listens. She can control her emotions to a certain extent. I love her ways. She's a great woman. Her clothes don't make her. She had self-control and that is a great thing to have.

Ladies, be proud of the way you think. Gentlemen, be happy for the way you love others. My people that are good in their heart are good people. Take pride in yourself more than your appearance.

Take pride in yourself more than your car. Take pride in yourself more than your house. Live your life the way God wants you to. Be powerful in spirit and you'll look amazing in appearance.

Do as is done. God sees your heart. Look for the good things and everyone before you decide if you like them. What is cute on the outside may be evil on the inside. What is cute on the outside may be rotten on the inside.

Keep your mind pure, keep your heart pure, and you are pure no matter what you look like. A wife and a husband are filled with something that the world can't see. That's why they were upgraded from a girlfriend to a wife and a boyfriend to a husband.

Never take for granted the heart of another because God doesn't. Remember, what God does is what is good.

1 Samuel v7

- *The Lord your God said to Samuel. Do not look at the appearance of someone. You men and women, look at people and see them based upon how*

they look, but the Lord looks at the person and sees
what's in their heart.-

AMEN

Chapter 9

Everyday

The people are only who they claim they are. If you say that you are evil, then you are evil. If you say that you are smart, then you are smart. I call myself powerful. I want you to give yourself a word.

A new word that will define you. Who you have become. Who you are now. After the test. After the trials and tribulations. After the experiences of life.

Who are you? What do you say you are? One word. What have you become? God is so powerful that he can transform whatever and whoever he wants. You are his, and he has given you the power to proclaim. State your status in life and live by it.

You are more than you were and you still have growth to be made, continue to grow. Continue to move closer to God and he will continue to pull you away from darkness. I see better days for you.

I see better days for me. I see better days for us. Do you? You should. I know that you are better than what you were, and I know that you are better than you know. I am the one that chooses. I am the one that honors.

I am the one that teaches. You arc better than you were because you believe. You are awesome because you have faith. You will do better because God will allow you to. Ask God for help and watch his power.

Tell God that you're sorry for the wrongs that you have done, and watch Him forgive you. He is yours to call on. Don't be afraid. He wants you to call on him.

He wants you to need him. He wants you to depend on him. He wants you to want his help. Don't let yourself let God down. Lose that ego and call on him and he will answer.

I love the life that God has given me. I love the life that God has shown me that I can have. Life is more than what I knew. Life is better than what I used to think it was. I have been taken away from the streets.

I have been taken away from the gangs, I have been taken away from poverty. I have more joy now than I did in my past because now I have accepted my gift.

I have accepted my path in life and continue to walk it in the righteousness that I have been shown to. The instructions that have been laid out to me, which have been written is what I use for help when I need it.

No man is perfect, but we all can become better than we were. Blessed is the man that can admit his flaws and ask for forgiveness. I was angry at my mother as a child until I asked God to forgive me.

I was angry at my father until I asked God to forgive me. Do you know why? Because the whole time that I was angry at them, I did not take accountability for the role that I played. I was angry at them, but not angry at myself.

Yes, I was a child. Yes, I wasn't the parent, but I still did wrong. I still did something that made them respond to me. I still didn't listen to them or their teachings. I was still disobeying their words.

I played a part in our awful relationship. Sometimes a man has to forgive himself for those bad relationships in order to move on in life. He has to give himself a chance to forgive, Give himself a chance to be forgiven. The world is so big that we can't see all of it.

When we are confined to our little space, our role in most situations gets blocked out because we never see the whole picture. We look at life through a small scope and always see the next person's role without seeing our own.

We always see the next person's flaws without taking the time out to notice our own. It's so easy to see what we are looking at, but it's not easy to see ourselves without looking into the mirror.

We don't just walk around with a mirror all day, so it's not as easy to reflect on ourselves. We have to take some real time to reflect on our wrongs. Our flaws. Our bad habits. Our addictions. Our reasons.

In order to fulfill our purpose. We have a purpose. I have a reason in life. You do too. You were angry because you allowed yourself to be. You weren't unhappy because you allowed yourself to be.

You were down because you laid down. This is not me condemning you. This is not you condemning you. This is you acknowledging your role in your life and accepting what you did to get there.

Accept your role, acknowledge your flaws and wrongdoings. Now ask God to forgive you. Before you can forgive someone else, you need to forgive yourself. Do your job to become better. Do your part of the healing process. Then let God handle the rest. He will, trust me.

You have to be willing. You have to admit it. You have to be able to. You have to be stable. Find stability in your mind to accept the lessons from God. Find stability in your mind to think better.

Your mind is the power. Your heart is what is viewed. God knows you because he created you. Ask

God to forgive you. Except what you did and then confess it. Except what you did, and then accept God's help.

Blessed is the one that listens. Blessed is the one that learns. Blessed is the one that acts God for what is needed. Believe that God has your back and you will see that he really does. Believe in the strength that he gives.

He has given you life. He has given you a chance. He has given you love. Trust me. God will forgive you. Now forgive yourself.

Ezekiel, chapter 36, verse 25-27.

- God said. This I will do. Sprinkle you with clean water and you will be clean from all of the

uncleanliness and from all of your wrongs. I will cleanse you. I'll give you a brand new heart and a brand new spirit to put inside of you. I will remove the old heart of stone from you and give you a heart of flesh. I will also put my spirit inside of you and make you walk in my way and make yourself careful to obey me and my rules.-

Chapter 10

Everyday

James Chapter 5, verse 7-9.

- Be patient.Until the Lord comes.Just as the farmer waits for his fruit.He is patient until his fruit grows early or late.You too have to be patient.Get your mind, body and spirit right, because the Lord is for sure coming.Be sure to not complain with your peers so you will not be judged.Because the judge is standing, waiting for you.-

In due time you will have everything that you want. In due time, you will receive everything that you desire. Life is playing out and you have something coming your way. You must be patient. You have to wait till it is time.

Every second counts. If you receive your big blessing. A week early, you may lose it due to the next man's jealousy. Next week, that man may be at work when you receive it. Today is not the time. Things may not happen as soon as you want them to, but trust me, it will come when it is time.

Set your alarm. Set your clock. Mark your calendar. Be realistic about your timing. Not all should happen fast. Not all should be rushed. When it is time to fly, your plane will depart. When it is time to cruise, your ship will sail.

When it is time to fall, the Peach will drop. There is an invisible clock that is ticking and you can't see it. You don't have the power to rush life. You don't have the power to rush blessings. Wait patiently because they come when needed.

Open your heart and feel the happiness flowing through it. Open your mind and let the positive thoughts accumulate. Think happy. Be happy. Love yourself in the process. Wait for the good to come without becoming filled with evil.

You are destined to be who you are destined to be. No matter how hard you try, you cannot rush what is destined to be. Have faith that what will happen is coming at will. I will be ready for it when it comes.

Say when it happens I will be ready. Don't act as if it is not coming out of eagerness. When we give up the ways of the past, we make life easier. When we walk in the light we walk away from the darkness.

Keep that light shining on me, is what I ask. Keep that light on me, is what I say. Keep those blessings coming, God. I'll be here when they come. I smile now instead of frowning. So should you. I laugh now instead of being angry.

I have replaced my old ways with the old ways written. The new ways to me are the old ways that were written. I just had to go back and read. The careless minds of my ex peers are the reasons why I no longer know them. The sinful ways of my ex peers are the reason why we no longer speak.

The harsh tongues of my ex-girlfriend is the reason why we no longer date.I have removed the bag that was in my life. To be honest, God did. Now I am comfortable within my heart.

Now I watched the blessings that God gave me. I have more time to appreciate them because I spend less time arguing. I have more time to give thanks because I spend less time partying. I have more time to learn from what is written because I spend less time playing around.

Now I am telling you what I have learned. The secret to life is simply to live .Nothing less than how you should. Stop living below yourself. You know what makes you smile?

You know what makes you happy. You know what makes you mad. Live your life according to what your heart feels. Keep your heart healthy. Keep your heart pure and your life will reflect that. Keep your peace, Be self-made happy, Have self-control. You are who you are and will be who you will be. You can't rush greatness. You cannot rush God's plan.

You have a lot in the works for you and you can't help but to be happy. Just be patient. You are a wonderful person that will receive your blessings.

Don't forget who you are, don't forget who you worship. Don't forget his powers, don't forget his capability and most importantly, don't forget his word.

James chapter 4, verse 10-15.

- Be sure to be humble before the Lord and he will accept you. Don't you dare say anything evil about others, because the one that does speak bad about his brother or tries to judge his brother is speaking bad against the law and it's truly judging the law. Remember that there is only one Lawgiver and Judge, and he is the one that can save and destroy. But who are you? You can't judge your neighbor. Pay attention. You who say today or tomorrow I will go here or do this or earn that amount of money, but you don't even know what will happen tomorrow. What are you? What do you truly

know? You are just here for a second and will be gone in another second. Instead, you need to say, if the Lord lets me, I will live and do this or that.-

AMEN

Made in the USA
Columbia, SC
25 May 2024